G00014936Z

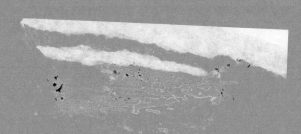

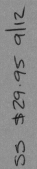

JSTOR

Journey of a Bowl of Cornflakes

John Malam

WILLIAM CLARKE COLLEGE LIBRARY
DELETED
FROM WCC LIBRARY
NF
664
MAL

www.raintreepublishers.co.uk
Visit our website to find out more information about Raintree books.

To order:
☎ Phone 0845 6044371
▤ Fax +44 (0) 1865 312263
▥ Email myorders@raintreepublishers.co.uk

Customers from outside the UK please telephone +44 1865 312262

Raintree is an imprint of Capstone Global Library Limited, a company incorporated in England and Wales having its registered office at 7 Pilgrim Street, London, EC4V 6LB – Registered company number: 6695582

Text © Capstone Global Library Limited 2012
First published in hardback in 2012
The moral rights of the proprietor have been asserted.

All rights reserved. No part of this publication may be reproduced in any form or by any means (including photocopying or storing it in any medium by electronic means and whether or not transiently or incidentally to some other use of this publication) without the written permission of the copyright owner, except in accordance with the provisions of the Copyright, Designs and Patents Act 1988 or under the terms of a licence issued by the Copyright Licensing Agency, Saffron House, 6–10 Kirby Street, London EC1N 8TS (www.cla.co.uk). Applications for the copyright owner's written permission should be addressed to the publisher.

Edited by Dan Nunn and Diyan Leake
Designed by Cynthia Della-Rovere
Original illustrations © Capstone Global Library Ltd 2012
Illustrated by Capstone Global Library Ltd
Picture research by Mica Brancic
Production by Alison Parsons
Originated by Capstone Global Library Ltd
Printed and bound in China by Leo Paper Products Ltd

ISBN 978 1 406 23933 1 (hardback)
16 15 14 13 12
10 9 8 7 6 5 4 3 2 1

British Library Cataloguing in Publication Data
Malam, John, 1957-
  Journey of a bowl of cornflakes.
  641.3'315-dc22
A full catalogue record for this book is available from the British Library.

Acknowledgements
The author and publishers are grateful to the following for permission to reproduce copyright material: Alamy pp. 16 (© Jeff Greenberg), 21 (© sciencephotos), 25 (© Art Directors & TRIP); © Capstone Publishers pp. 18 (Karon Dubke), 27 (Karon Dubke); Corbis pp. 20 (© Peter Yates), 28 (© the food passionates); © Dusko Matic pp. 15, 19; Getty Images pp. 12 (© Aurora/Tom Sperduto), 22 (© Dmitry Kalinovsky), 23 (© Photodisc/Monty Rakusen); © Kellogg's p. 14; Science Photo Library p. 26 (© Peter Menzel); Shutterstock pp. 3 (© Picsfive), 4 (© Brooke Becker), 5 (oats, © Sinelyov), 5 (corn, © Giuseppe R), 5 (rice, © Imageman), 5 (wheat, © Imageman), 6 (© Tom Fakler), 7 (© Bandy), 9 (© Foto011), 10 (© Steve Heap), 11 (© Tish1), 13 (© Africa Studio), 17 (© Picsfive), 24 (© Eric Gevaert), 29 top (© Giuseppe R), 29 bottom (© Brooke Becker), 31 top (© Foto011), 31 middle (© Africa Studio), 31 bottom (© Picsfive).

Cover photographs of a maize field (© Tish1) and a bowl of cornflakes (© Oliver Hoffmann) reproduced with permission of Shutterstock.

Every effort has been made to contact copyright holders of material reproduced in this book. Any omissions will be rectified in subsequent printings if notice is given to the publisher.

Disclaimer
All the internet addresses (URLs) given in this book were valid at the time of going to press. However, due to the dynamic nature of the internet, some addresses may have changed, or sites may have changed or ceased to exist since publication. While the author and publisher regret any inconvenience this may cause readers, no responsibility for any such changes can be accepted by either the author or the publisher.

Contents

Some words are shown in bold, **like this**. You can find out what they mean by looking in the Glossary.

What's for breakfast?

Breakfast is the first meal of the day. You eat breakfast in the morning, soon after you wake up. Breakfast gives your body the energy it needs for a good start to the day.

Does your breakfast cereal look like one of these?

maize

oats

rice

wheat

Many people eat **cereal** at breakfast time.
Most breakfast cereals are made from the
grains of plants such as wheat, oats, rice,
and **maize**.

Corn to cornflake

Cornflakes are one type of breakfast **cereal**. They are made from the **grains** of the **maize** plant. Maize is also known as corn. This is why the cereal it makes is called cornflakes.

The part that the corn grains grow on is called an ear.

Cornflakes start off as soft grains of corn growing in farmers' fields. They end up as crunchy cereal that people eat with milk at breakfast time.

Growing the corn

Corn grows in many countries. Most corn grows in the United States. Farmers **sow** their fields with corn seeds every year.

■ US Corn Belt state

This map shows the areas where corn grows in the United States.

8

Corn seeds grow into tall plants.

Each plant has one or two ears of corn. There are hundreds of soft, juicy **grains** or **kernels** of yellow corn on each ear.

Harvesting the corn

The sun warms the ears of corn. The **kernels** become hard and dry. Farmers **harvest** the sun-dried corn kernels in September. Only the best kernels are used for cornflakes.

This farmer is harvesting a field of corn.

A combine harvester is a big machine.

Some farmers drive a combine harvester through the fields of corn. The combine cuts the ears off the corn plants. Then it takes the kernels off the ears.

From farm to mill

Farmers sell the dried **kernels** to a corn **mill**. Lorries take the kernels from the farm to the mill. At the mill, the kernels are cleaned and sorted.

This farmer is unloading his corn harvest so that it is ready to take to a corn mill.

Each grit of corn will become a cornflake.

When the kernels are clean, they go into a milling or grinding machine. It breaks them into small, hard pieces called **grits**.

From mill to factory

The corn **mill** sells the corn **grits** to a cornflake **factory**. At the factory, the hard grits are put into a **steam** cooker for about one hour. Then the grits are dried in a machine.

There are many big buildings at the cornflake factory.

The grits have changed shape and become flakes.

The dried grits go to a machine that squeezes them between two large rollers. When they come out of the rolling machine, they look like cornflakes for the first time.

Toasting the flakes

The flakes of corn are still quite soft when they leave the rolling machine. They are toasted inside a big oven to turn them into crunchy cornflakes. Thousands of flakes of corn are tossed around inside the oven.

There are switches to control the machines in the cornflake **factory**.

These are freshly toasted cornflakes, straight from the oven.

The oven is very hot. It is much hotter than an oven at home. It only takes a few seconds to toast the flakes. The oven crisps them all over until they are a golden brown colour.

Adding flavour

A **conveyor belt** takes the toasted cornflakes to a big drum. Inside the drum, the cornflakes are sprayed all over with sugar, flavours, **minerals**, and **vitamins**.

Cornflakes get their taste from the flavours that are added to them.

These are cornflakes on a conveyor belt.

conveyor belt

Another conveyor belt takes the cornflakes to the bagging area. A machine weighs out the right amount of cornflakes for each bag. The cornflakes drop into a bag. The top of the bag is sealed. It takes just two seconds to fill a bag with cornflakes and seal it.

Into boxes

The filled cornflake liners move to a packing machine. This puts them into boxes. The boxes are made out of thin card and have the **brand** of the cornflakes on them. There are lots of different brands of cornflakes.

The boxes leave the packing machine when they are full of cornflakes.

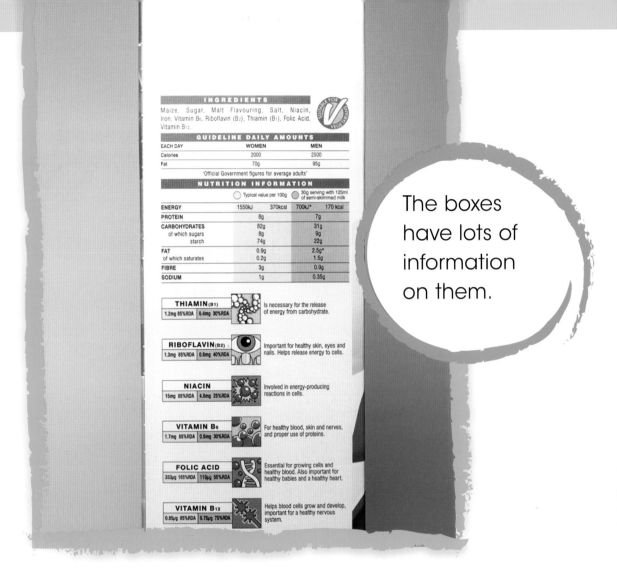

INGREDIENTS

Maize, Sugar, Malt Flavouring, Salt, Niacin, Iron, Vitamin B6, Riboflavin (B2), Thiamin (B1), Folic Acid, Vitamin B12.

SUITABLE FOR VEGETARIANS

GUIDELINE DAILY AMOUNTS

EACH DAY	WOMEN	MEN
Calories	2000	2500
Fat	70g	95g

'Official Government figures for average adults'

NUTRITION INFORMATION

	Typical value per 100g		30g serving with 125ml of semi-skimmed milk	
ENERGY	1550kJ	370kcal	700kJ*	170 kcal
PROTEIN	8g		7g	
CARBOHYDRATES	82g		31g	
of which sugars	8g		9g	
starch	74g		22g	
FAT	0.9g		2.5g*	
of which saturates	0.2g		1.5g	
FIBRE	3g		0.9g	
SODIUM	1g		0.35g	

THIAMIN (B1)		Is necessary for the release of energy from carbohydrate.
1.2mg 85%RDA	0.4mg 30%RDA	

RIBOFLAVIN (B2)		Important for healthy skin, eyes and nails. Helps release energy to cells.
1.3mg 85%RDA	0.6mg 40%RDA	

NIACIN		Involved in energy-producing reactions in cells.
15mg 85%RDA	4.6mg 25%RDA	

VITAMIN B6		For healthy blood, skin and nerves, and proper use of proteins.
1.7mg 85%RDA	0.5mg 30%RDA	

FOLIC ACID		Essential for growing cells and healthy blood. Also important for healthy babies and a healthy heart.
333µg 165%RDA	110µg 55%RDA	

VITAMIN B12		Helps blood cells grow and develop, important for a healthy nervous system.
0.85µg 85%RDA	0.75µg 75%RDA	

The boxes have lots of information on them.

Each brand has its own design for the box. There is information about the **ingredients** in the cornflakes. There is a "Best Before" date. It means that it is best to eat the cornflakes before that date.

In the warehouse

The boxes of cornflakes are packed into large cardboard cartons. Each carton holds lots of boxes. The cartons are sent to a **warehouse**.

There are lots of shelves in a warehouse.

This lorry is being loaded with cartons of cornflakes.

The cartons of cornflakes are stacked on high shelves in the warehouse. Lorries go to the warehouse and collect them. The cornflakes are loaded on to the lorries.

On the road

The lorries may have to go a long way. They drive to supermarkets and shops.

These lorries have arrived at a big supermarket.

24

The cartons of cornflakes are unloaded and opened. People working at the supermarket put the boxes of cornflakes on to the shelves.

At the supermarket

Shoppers choose which **brand** of cornflakes they want. There are lots to choose from! There are also other **cereals** made from other **grains**.

Shoppers take the box of cornflakes to the checkout along with their other shopping. They pay for it and take it home.

Just add milk!

At breakfast time, you put some cornflakes into a bowl. Pour fresh milk over them and they are ready to eat.

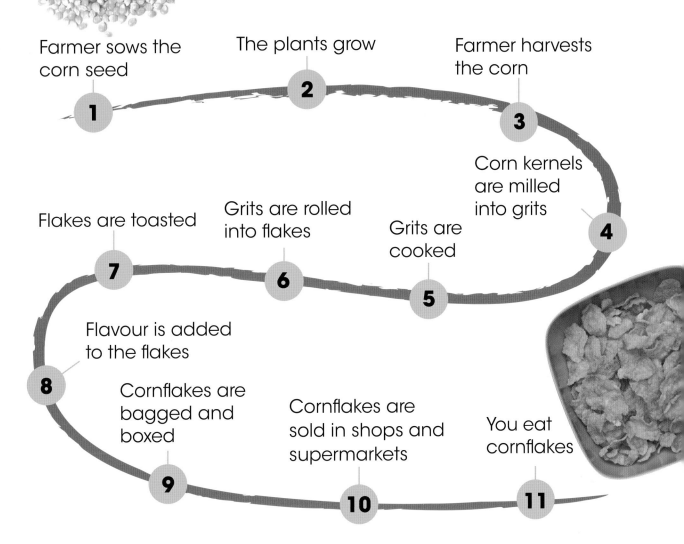

Farmer sows the corn seed — **1**

The plants grow — **2**

Farmer harvests the corn — **3**

Corn kernels are milled into grits — **4**

Grits are cooked — **5**

Grits are rolled into flakes — **6**

Flakes are toasted — **7**

Flavour is added to the flakes — **8**

Cornflakes are bagged and boxed — **9**

Cornflakes are sold in shops and supermarkets — **10**

You eat cornflakes — **11**

From start to finish, it takes between six and eight months to make cornflakes. Somewhere in the world, a farmer is growing corn right now. That corn may become the cornflakes that you eat in a few months.

Glossary

brand name of particular make of goods

cereal breakfast food made from grains

conveyor belt rubber surface that moves along, carrying things on it

factory building where things are made

grain small, hard seed of a cereal plant

grit broken up pieces of corn grains

harvest gather in the crops

ingredient part used in a mixture; one of the foods in a recipe

kernel single whole grain of corn

maize another word for corn

mill factory where corn grains are prepared

mineral something found in meat, beans, and other foods, which the human body needs to stay healthy

sow plant a seed

steam water that is in the form of a gas because it is very hot

vitamin something found in fruit, vegetables, and other foods, which the human body needs to stay healthy

warehouse building where things are stored

Cornflake quiz

1. What plants do corn kernels grow on? (see page 6)

2. What colour are corn kernels? (see page 9)

3. What are corn kernels broken down into? (see page 13)

4. How long does it take to toast cornflakes? (see page 17)

5. What do you pour over cornflakes at breakfast time? (see page 28)

Find out more

This is an animated guide to how cornflakes are made:
www.kelloggs.co.uk/whatson/provenance

Here is another animated guide:
urbanext.illinois.edu/corn/03.html

Answers to quiz

1. maize plants, 2. yellow, 3. grits, 4. a few seconds, 5. milk

Index